What Am I?

What Kind of MAMMAL AM I?

Taylor Farley

TABLE OF CONTENTS

What Kind of Mammal Am I? ... 2

Glossary 22

Index 23

A Crabtree Seedlings Book

CRABTREE
Publishing Company
www.crabtreebooks.com

What Kind of Mammal Am I?

I am the largest mammal on Earth, and I live in the sea.

What kind of mammal am I?

A blue whale

I have both black and white fur, and I eat bamboo.

What kind of mammal am I?

A panda

I am the only mammal that can truly fly.

What kind of mammal am I?

A bat

I have tough, wrinkled skin and live in a herd.

What kind of mammal am I?

An elephant

I am the only mammal with a shell.

What kind of mammal am I?

19

An armadillo

Glossary

armadillo (ar-muh-DIL-oh): Armadillos use their sharp claws for digging up insects and grubs for food.

bat (BAT): Bats hang upside down when they sleep.

blue whale (BLOO WAYL): Blue whales make sounds that other blue whales can hear up to 1,000 miles (1,600 kilometers) away.

elephant (EL-uh-fuhnt): Elephants are the largest land mammals on Earth.

panda (PAN-duh): Wild pandas live in the mountains of China. Pandas are a type of bear.

Index

Earth 2
fly 10
fur 6
herd 14
shell 18
skin 14

What Is a Mammal?
A mammal is a warm-blooded animal with a backbone. Female mammals produce milk to feed their babies. Nearly all mammals give birth to live babies. Only a few types of mammals lay eggs.

School-to-Home Support for Caregivers and Teachers

This book helps children grow by letting them practice reading. Here are a few guiding questions to help the reader build his or her comprehension skills. Possible answers appear here in red.

Before Reading
- **What do I think this book is about?** I think this book is about different kinds of mammals. I think this book is about the places where mammals live.
- **What do I want to learn about this topic?** I want to learn more about what mammals like to eat. I want to learn why an animal is called a mammal.

During Reading
- **I wonder why…** I wonder why bats hang upside down. I wonder why pandas like to eat bamboo.
- **What have I learned so far?** I have learned that armadillos are the only mammals with a shell. I have learned that armadillos use their sharp claws to dig for food.

After Reading
- **What details did I learn about this topic?** I have learned that blue whales make sounds that other blue whales can hear up to 1,000 miles (1,600 km) away. I have learned that elephants are the largest land mammals on Earth.
- **Read the book again and look for the glossary words.** I see the word *panda* on page 8, and the word *elephant* on page 17. The other glossary words are found on pages 22 and 23.

Library and Archives Canada Cataloguing in Publication

CIP available at Library and Archives Canada

Library of Congress Cataloging-in-Publication Data

CIP available at Library of Congress

Crabtree Publishing Company
www.crabtreebooks.com   1-800-387-7650

Written by: Taylor Farley
Print coordinator: Katherine Berti

Print book version produced jointly with Blue Door Education in 2023   Printed in the U.S.A./072022/CG20220201

Content produced and published by Blue Door Education, Melbourne Beach FL USA. This title Copyright Blue Door Education. All rights reserved. No part of this book may be reproduced or utilized in any form or by any means, electronic or mechanical including photocopying, recording, or by any information storage and retrieval system without permission in writing from the publisher.

PHOTO CREDITS:
whale tail © Gerckens-Photo-Hamburg; blue whale © Andrew Sutton; panda page 7 © Kevin Bluer; panda page 9 © Pascale Gueret; elephant closeup © GR92100; elephants © Matej Kastelic; bat © Nuwat Phansuwan; armadillo © Tim Zurowski. All photos from www.Shutterstock.com

Published in the United States
Crabtree Publishing
347 Fifth Ave.
Suite 1402-145
New York, NY 10016

Published in Canada
Crabtree Publishing
616 Welland Ave.
St. Catharines, Ontario
L2M 5V6